VERSE FOR THE JOURNEY

Poems on the Wandering Life

Translated from the German

by

William Ruleman

CEDAR SPRINGS BOOKS

Published by Cedar Springs Books, 2014, 2018.

ISBN-13: 978-0692320822

ISBN-10: 0692320822

Acknowledgments

The author is grateful to the following publications, in which some of the poems in this book first appeared:

The Poetry Church for "Verses to a Little Child," "None Has Rued It Yet," "The Happy Wanderer," & "Walking Tour"

O My News International for "Two Wanderers"

Open Writing for "A Winter Evening"

TABLE OF CONTENTS

PREFACE

The impulse to wander: is it not a natural trait of our species? Indeed, where would we be without it? Still in caves or trees, most likely. Polyphemus, the one-eyed Cyclops in Homer's *The Odyssey*, never goes anywhere; and he is ignorant, bigoted—and downright mean. True, Odysseus's own sea-roaming tends toward the frivolous. His whimsical wanderlust ends up costing the lives of all of his men. It also imperils his Ithacan home, the blessedness of his long-lasting marriage to faithful and ever-patient Penelope. Yes, wandering can be dangerous. Yet it can have its positive side, and what I intend to stress in this, the first of a series of books on the subject, is just that. I hope to present the theme with all the sense of delight to be found in these "Verses to a Little Child" composed by the Austrian poet Hugo von Hofmannsthal (1874-1929):

Your rosy feet grow for you
To seek the lands of the sun:
They're open, those sunny lands!
The air of a thousand years
Still clings to silent trees;
The unexhausted seas
Are ever, forever there.
On the fringe of eternal woods
Will you deign to share with the toad
The milk from the wooden cup?
'Twill be such a merry meal,
The stars will nearly fall in!
On the shores of eternal seas,
You'll quickly find a friend:
The dolphin, good and kind.
He'll leap to you on the dry land,
And should he at times not show,
The infinite winds shall still
The tears welling up within.
The old, exalted times
Remain in the lands of the sun—
Forever and ever, still!
With secret might, the sun

Will form your rosy feet
To tread her eternal land.

To wander: is it not to return to the wondering heart and soul of a child? And since the impulse, once whetted, never ends, is it not seek the eternal? Hofmannsthal, for certain, knew the impulse, and also knew that every trail, no matter how often explored, remains forever new. Whether others have trodden the same earthly path is of no consequence: the important thing is the journey that we ourselves take, the things that we learn for ourselves on that path. It is in that spirit that I have composed and compiled the translations in this book. All are of poems in the German Romantic tradition of *wandern*, which celebrates the notion of roaming freely with no strict design or end, though some of the poems, such as Maria Luise Weissmann's "The Wandering Staff" and Hedwig Lachmann's "In the Evening" call the tradition into question, whereas Eichendorff's "The Stranger " and "The Homecoming" suggest what may ensue if one strays from home too long.

These translations are of poems by German Romantic poets, and other German-language poets working within—and responding to—the Romantic tradition. I did not include poems by their English contemporaries, whose poetry I have read and taught every year for decades now and continue to love. My reason for this has to do with what I sought to emphasize in this volume. Certainly Wordsworth, Shelley, Byron, Keats, and other English Romantics enjoyed "walking tours," and their poetry often speaks of their experiences on these tours—especially of their inspired responses to nature. Yet when I began to read and translate the German Romantics, what I noticed was that they tended to focus more on *hiking* for its own sake, or, in a more general sense, on "wandering." So I aimed to share with readers familiar with the English Romantics but not with their German counterparts a sense of what I see as a somewhat different focus.

To be sure, the whole notion of "wandering" does go hand in hand with the high Romantic yearning to regain, or achieve for the very first time, a sense of communion with the natural world. And it is imperative that we remember this. For, though we still claim to treasure this aim today, too often the quest to compete with other hikers, to set a record, to conquer nature by seeing how far we can hike or how high,

7

interferes and leads to unhappiness, to alienation from ourselves, from our fellow human beings, and from our world. For that reason, a work like this is important. It helps to show us how to recover a sense of the joys that can be found in the sheer abandon to *wandern*. While not intended as comprehensive, it will, ideally, incite the reader to seek the delights of wandering on his or her own. It should also serve as a handy companion for those already embarked on their own adventures in wandering.

A BLESSING FOR WANDERERS

(Johann Wolfgang von Goethe)

The years of wandering have begun today.
Each step the wanderer takes is fraught with danger.
He certainly has no wish to sing or pray,
And yet the moment his path turns trickier, stranger
(The moment mist clouds all below, above)
He enters his own heart—that, and the heart of love.

MIGNON

(Johann Wolfgang von Goethe)

Do you know the land where the lemon trees bloom
And the oranges glow in the dark leaves' gloom
And a mild wind blows from a deep blue sky
And the myrtle stands still and the laurel looms high?
Do you know it then?
                    O hear, o hear!
I yearn to go with you there, my dear!

Do you know the house with its pillars that hold
The roof, the halls, the rooms gleaming gold
Whose marble statues stand staring at me:
"What have they done to you, child? O see!"
Do you know it then?
                    That house so true?
I yearn to go with you there, I do.

Do you know the heights and the bridge, cloud-kissed;
The mule that seeks its way in the mist;
The dungeon caves of the old dragon's brood;
The plunging crag 'neath the flood's plenitude?
Do you know it then?
                    O, that is where
Our pathway leads! O, let us go *there*!

DEDICATION

(Johann Wolfgang von Goethe)

The morning came; its footsteps scared away
The gentle sleep that quietly clung to me
So that, departing my silent hut for day,
I climbed the mountain with new serenity;
With every step, I thrilled in each new spray
Of dew-filled blooms, which drooped quite gracefully;
The new day rose with boundless new delight,
And all was refreshed, refreshing my soul and sight.

And as I climbed, a mist, in streaks, rose softly,
Softly forth, from the river in the meadows,
Effaced itself and melted to flow around me,
And soared as if winged up round my head and rose
Till I no longer could savor the scenery;
The vista lay hid from me as if by floes
Of fog. I saw myself surrounded by clouds,
Confined, alone, in twilight's shrouds.

At once the sun appeared to rend the fog's veil,
Permitting clarity to pierce its nest.
And here it fluttered down, a sinking sail;
And there it rose and broke round wood and crest.
And how I hoped to be the first to hail
A sun now doubly lovely, doubly blessed!
Long ere this airy strife declined,
A glow surrounded me and struck me blind.

A heartfelt urge in time emboldened me
To try to see again, though I could dare
No more than rapid glances furtively;
For all around me seemed to flash and flare.
Then, borne upon the clouds to me,
A woman like a goddess hovered there;
No lovelier image shone in all my days
Than she who lingered there, with piercing gaze.

11

"Do you not know me?" she uttered with a calm
Of voice that flowed with love profound and true:
"For it was I who poured the purest balm
Upon life's many hurtful wounds for you.
You know me well, to whom, with ne'er a qualm,
Your striving heart was bound in each sinew.
Did I not see the boy already yearning
For me with tears hot, bright, and fiercely burning?"

I called out "Yes!" and sank down blissfully
To earth. "Indeed, I have long since felt your care.
You gave me peace when passion restlessly
Gnawed through my youthful limbs; and you were there,
As with celestial feathers, lovingly
To cool my brow in day's insistent glare;
You gave me the best gifts of the earth;
Alone through you do I wish peace and mirth!"

I name you not, though often *hear* you named
By many, and each one calls you his;
And every eye believes that it is aimed
Toward you; and yet for most, in spite of this,
Your rays prove painful. Straying, friends I claimed,
But knowing you, find solitude my bliss;
I must, alone, exult in my delight;
I must conceal and lock away your light."

She smiled and said: "You see how wise
And needful it was to show so little to you?
You are scarcely safe from the most outrageous lies;
Scarcely lord are you of your retinue
Of childish desires; you exalt yourself to the skies
And yet neglect the duties a man should do!"
How truly different are you from all the others?
Know yourself; live in peace with the world and your brothers."

"Forgive me!" I cried. "I really meant well. Should
I not have? Indeed, have I opened my eyes in vain?
A happy will is living in my blood;
I know completely the worth of your gifts' domain!

There grows in me—for others—the noble good;
I can and *will* not bury my talents again!
Why on earth did I so seek and yearn
The way, if not to guide my brothers in turn?"

And as I spoke, the lofty being inclined
Toward me with sympathetic tolerance;
Her eyes reflected my own heart and mind—
Where I had failed and where known excellence.
She smiled. I was already healed, I thrilled to find;
My spirit rose with an inner confidence
Toward new joys; now I found that I
Could move to look on her from closer by.

"I know you—know your every frailty—
Know what gleams inside you, good and true!"
She said (I hear her speak eternally):
"Receive here what I have long intended for you!
Naught can be lacking to he who is lucky and happy,
Who takes the gift with a soul of tranquil hue
Spun forth from morning haze and sun's bright brand:
The veil of poetry from truth's own hand."

And when it grows too warm at midday for
Your friends and you, toss it into the air! For then
The evening breeze will rustle, cool once more
And flowers' spicy fragrance breathe again.
The blast of earthly fears will cease its roar,
The grave be changed to a bed of cloud, for when
Every rough wave of life is pacified,
The day will be lovely, the night as bright as noontide."

So come then, friends, when out upon your ways,
Life's burden presses more and more heavily,
Whenever a fresh-renewed blessing adorns your days
With flowers, and golden fruits that are heavenly,
We'll go united to meet the next day's gaze!
So we shall live and walk in all jollity.
And then, when our grandchildren someday shall mourn our going,
Our love shall remain for them, a joy ever-flowing.

WANDERING

(Ludwig Tieck)

Good day! The sun now calls you out;
The world of God's at hand!
Stroll the glad fields all about;
Wander through the land!
The stream stays not at rest, my friend:
On its waters race;
Hear the happy rushing wind?
It roars from place to place.

The moon glides here and there with glee;
The sun moves on its course
From highest heights down to the sea
With untiring force;
But you, man, always stay at home:
Don't you long for change?
Explore that grove and freshly roam;
Enjoy the far and strange.

Where your luck will bloom, who knows?
So seek it: don't hold back!
The evening comes, the morning goes;
Tread forth on your track!
The heavens stretch around so wide,
Fragrant with love's fruit,
That all hearts will know joy inside,
Fulfilling their pursuit.

NONE HAS RUED IT YET

(Ludwig Tieck)

No one who has flown his way
Throughout the world in youth
On racing steed can ever say
That he has suffered ruth.

Mountains, leas,
Woods forlorn,
Ladies please
Him with their bold
Attire and gold
And all the lovely forms they adorn.

Shapes flee and flow
Miraculously;
Wishes glow
In his youthful soul exuberantly.

Fame strews roses
In his way;
Loving poses,
Laurels, roses
Lead him to ever higher day.

Joys surround him;
Envying him,
His enemies fall;
Sans pride or whim,
The hero selects the best girl of all.

And mountains, fields,
And lonely woods
Call home the boy.
His parents in tears
(Ah, their yearnings, fears)
Rejoin him with the loveliest joy.

When years have fled,
Son by his bed,
He feels the need
To show where he bled:
Bravery's meed.
Hence age stays young and bright:
In dusk still gleams a light.

A FRESH FARING-FORTH

(Joseph von Eichendorff)

Warm winds flowing through the blue,
Horn blasts shooting through the wood—
Spring, oh spring, it must be you!
The gleam of brave eyes means much good;
Confusion mounts, its motley glow
Waxes manic, stirs your blood,
Lures you into the lovely flow
Of this world's wild and magic flood.

And I don't want to shrink from its call!
I want to fare forth down that stream,
Wind-propelled far from you all,
Blissfully blinded by its gleam!
A thousand luring voices cry;
Aurora wafts, ablaze, on high;
On! Don't let me ask, my friend,
Where this journey's going to end!

TRAVEL SONG

(Joseph von Eichendorff)

I go my way as if in dreams,
My heart is so at rest;
Every path is straight, it seems,
The weather of the best.

Where'er my way might make me stray,
The sky's my canopy;
The sun re-arises every day;
The stars watch over me.

And whether early or late I find
The end toward which I plod,
I know that I will *never* find
I'm lost from your world, dear God!

THE HAPPY WANDERER

(Joseph von Eichendorff)

God sends into the wide, wide world
The one whom he would grant with good;
In mountain, stream, in field and wood,
He'll show him all His wonders unfurled.

The sluggish who lie at home in bed
Are not refreshed by the sun's glad rise,
Know only cradles, babies' cries,
Worries, burdens, dearth of bread.

The brooks spring from the mountain height,
The larks whir overhead with joy . . .
Sing too! Why not—as when a boy—
Throat full, chest puffed, with all my might?

I'll simply let my dear God reign.
He, who would maintain His mark
On forest, field, on sky, on lark—
On *earth*—best rules my small domain!

WANDERING FOR EVERYONE

(Joseph von Eichendorff)

From vale to fog-veiled peak
As far as one can see,
In bloom now, every tree,
And wanderers start to seek

(with Poet in the lead)
The chasms' gushing lair,
The stream upon the mead,
The larks high in the air.

And those in the vale, distracted,
Corrupted by gloomy care,
He'd like to see attracted
To roaming here and there.

And then his song rings down
From the mountain to the vale,
And his brothers in the town
Are homesick and struck pale.

Then the world fills with cheer
And goes on a roaming spree,
His loved one among them there
Nodding secretly.

And on the precipice,
And on the grassy mead,
With endless shouts and bliss,
Now let the roaming proceed!

LONGING

(Joseph von Eichendorff)

Stars glow with golden light.
Alone at the window I stand
And hear, far off in the night,
Posthorns in the silent land.
My heart flares in my breast,
And secretly my delight
Is to ride along with the rest
This splendid summer night!

Two lads go wandering
Past on a mountain slope,
And as they roam, they sing
Songs of joy and hope—
Of dizzying mountain chasms
Where the forests murmur so;
Of springs that plunge in spasms
Where the woodlands' night winds blow.

They sing of sculptured stone,
Of marble chalices,
Of gardens overgrown,
Of moonlit palaces
Where girls in windows listen
When the lilt of lutes delights
And the fountains drowsily glisten
In the splendid summer nights.

WALKING TOUR

(Eduard Mörike)

On fresh-hewn staff I lean
When early (close to dawn)
I roam woods' gold or green,
Up the hills and down.
Then, as leaf-veiled bird
Sings and is bestirred,
Or gold grapes feel the kiss
Of spirits, ghosts of bliss
In early morning sun:
So my old Adam will know
Fall, spring's feverish glow,
God-encouraged,
Never-disparaged
Primal bliss of Eden.

So what strict teachers proclaim
Of your old *evil* Adam—not true!
For still you love and praise,
Sing and ever raise
As on days made ever new
Your Creator-Sustainer's name.

O might it be granted me
That my whole life could be
Such a morning's fling
In the light sweat of wandering!

ON A RAMBLE

(Eduard Mörike)

I enter a friendly little town;
The streets wear evening's glowing red gown.
Then, through a window open to
A meadow now in fragrant flower,
I hear gold bells ring soft but true.
And *one* voice seems a nightingales' choir,
To make the blossoms quiver
And the breezes shiver
And all the roses shine with heightened fire.

I stop astounded, anxious with delight.
How I came to be here by the gate tonight
I myself do not really know.
The world shines here with such a rich glow!
The sky is surging in crimson turmoil;
Behind me, the city in golden haze;
How the mill clatters, the brook's waters roil!
I feel as if drunk or led astray;
O Muse, you have touched my heart today
With a breath of love's mild ways!

WANDERING IN THE MOUNTAINS

(Nikolaus Lenau)

Memory

To me you were really true; my dear
Companion. Come, my lovely day:
Draw closer once more to me over here
That I might enjoy you, if I may.

Departure

The happy face of heaven burned
Already from the day's first kiss,
And via the morning star, it turned
To the night and said farewell. With this,

I reached out for my walking staff
And said to my host: "May God reward
This place of rest." Then, with a laugh,
I stepped out into the world of the Lord.

The Lark

The bees gladly buzzed toward the sweet loot there
On the bridge that spanned the meadows;
The lark then strewed her songs on the air,
On the path, in the sun, in the shadows.

The Forest of Oaks

I stepped inside the holy gloom
Of a wood of oaks, where, soft and mild,
A little brook whispered under spring bloom
Like the prayer of a little child.

As the forest murmured mysteriously,
I felt seized by a sweet sort of threat,
As if the wood might confide to me

Something my heart should not know yet;

As if wishing, in secret, to show me here
The love of God, His thought, His will:
And then it seemed to start in fear
Of His nearness—and grew still.

The Herdsman

Far from the wood I already go,
Along a mountain wall steep and sheer;
And yet I often look down below
Where the last treetops disappear.

A cow strays on the meadows' brink;
A herdsman sheltered by pine boughs above
Him clings silently, with the bell's soft clink,
To the image of his little love.

Solitude

Now I see herdsman, herd no more:
My escort, only a little air;
The steep path grows ever steeper before
Me, loneliness mounting everywhere.

There, from a crag-encrusted grot,
The spring, with fearful shout and spray,
Leaps, dividing the frightful spot,
Down, on down to friendly green May.

Life's last signs now disappear:
Green leaf, bird song grow scant as one's breath;
Even the path seems to tremble here,
Caught 'twixt wall and Gorge of Death.

Come, God-denier, and feel Him now:
Your crime will plumb the abyss with its view
Of death more deeply on this steep brow,

Before this wall that looms over you!

The Expanse

I saw them now, the mountain's heights,
Which looked down so defiantly;
Nature, pierced by your lure of delights,
How my heart beat loudly, abundantly!

The plain spanned forth quite cozily
On and on, through endless lands
With towers, fields, and woods' greenery
And streams embroidered with colorful bands.

At once, it resolutely rose
Up to the sky with bolder force;
Its peaks, laced round with ice and snows,
Checked the clouds upon their course.

Soon I fixed my eyes, joy-drunk,
Upon the wild and jagged height;
Soon my soul, in silence, had sunk
Upon the mysterious distant sight.

The dark and far-off lands convey
Their sister, Longing, so I stir—
Take up my staff, resume my way
On up the mountain to her, to her.

How many a marvelous magic spell
Nature could concoct up there;
How many a worthy one, as well,
Whose hand I could shake, might live up there!

The Thunder

Still ever a deep and silent trance
Lies round the heights, and yet, with a wail,
The wind soars up in manic dance
Upon the thunder's rushing trail.

The gloomy train of clouds shakes up,
With muffled sounds, the heavens' vault:
With heated urging, rage takes up
In turn the nightly flight of thought.

The sky roars forth his quarrel now;
The veins of lightning start to glow;
With ire upon his darkened brow,
The earthly terror starts to grow.

Rain races in a noisy sheet
With trees the storm breaks into pieces;
The stream resounds, foams at my feet;
The thunder all too slowly ceases.

The storm then lets its mad wings sink;
The rain then sighs and grows sedate;
I see light from a small hut wink
And hasten to its gate.

An old man smiles, comes up to me,
Thoughtfully offering me his hand,
Then lifts it to the wild and free
Blessing flowing from Heaven's land;

And deep down in my heart, I feel
That raging godly din no more,
For from the west, Love seems to deal
Me dalliance from thunder's roar.

And, tired, I drink a soothing drink;
And where the silence calls, I creep
Out to the barn, commence to sink
Into the fragrant hay and sleep.

And what has thrilled me on my way
I dream of now, in sleep that's lovely;
And as I dreamed there in the hay,
I hear the rain pat on the roof above me.

How sweet to dream in hay's soft nest
When rain is gently plopping down;
So may it be the day I rest
In open coffin, friends' tears dropping down.

The Evening

By now the clouds had drifted on;
The sun was gleaming, sinking low;
And on the hills, a rainbow shone
As I gathered myself to go.

I reached out for my walking staff,
Gave my host my gratitude
For the resting place and gentle quaff,
And set off through dusk's quietude.

THE STRANGER

(Joseph von Eichendorff)

The evening bells in the village were already ringing;
The tired little birds had tucked in for the night;
And in the meadow, the crickets alone were singing,
While forests murmured from every mountain height,
When, through the waves of corn, a wanderer came
Who seemed from distant lands, for none knew his name.

Before his door, with leaves and blooms o'erhead,
A man invited him to glad repose.
The young man's wife brought wine and grapes and bread,
And so he sat down where the last gold glows;
And smiling, half shy, half in devilry,
A curly toddler climbed up on his knee.

It seemed he might have been in that village once,
And yet the clothes he wore were odd and strange;
You read a fiery script in his countenance
Like lightning on a distant mountain range.
And they were filled with dread when they met his eye,
For it was like looking into endless sky.

And now, as cool shadows spelled the close of day,
How wonderfully the lovely guest could speak
Of Vesuvius, smoking over a ruined Pompeii,
Of seas where singing swans glide, soft and sleek,
And in whose depths, crystal islands bloom,
And bells sound deep within its cavernous gloom.

"You've seen a great deal," the landlord said to his guest.
"Do you want to roam forever? I beg your pardon,
But here you can live in pleasure like the rest,
Have your own hearth and tend your own little garden . . .
The neighbors' daughters, you'll find, have riches galore!
Stay here! No need to be alone anymore."

At that, the wanderer stood up. Already star

On star over the still dark land now bloomed and burned.
"God bless you," he said. "But I must travel far
To reach my native land." Then, as he turned,
Celestial sounds came from the glade. Out here,
They'd never seen a night so starry and clear.

THE WANDERER

(Justinus Kerner)

The roads I travel on,
Homeless and alone,
Seem remote and strange.
Where I wish to stay
Seems all too far away,
E'er beyond my range.

These towns and fields I spy
Are strangers to my eye,
The castles dead and dumb.
Yet distant mountains roam,
And in their hands my home:
The endless dawn to come.

A WANDERER'S SONG

(Alfons Petzold)

Here sings every stone,
Every stem and tree:
"Wanderer, your own
Homeland's mere reverie.

Neither here nor there
Deep in selected sod
But here, there, everywhere
Blooms your world and God."

TWO WANDERERS

(Friedrich Hebbel)

A mute one makes his way through the land.
To him, the Lord has thought to confide
A word he cannot fathom, name—
A word that he can but proclaim
To one he has not yet descried.

A deaf one makes his way through the land.
The Lord has hailed him in his flight—
One whose hearing's congealed,
One whose lips are sealed
Till another is in his sight.

Then the dumb one will speak,
The deaf one hear him right.
He'll mine the mother lode
Of God's dark, secret code;
And they'll move toward morning's light.

In order to find them both,
Good people, pray and pray.
Though each still wanders alone,
When the other's presence is known,
The world will have its day.

MORNING WANDERING

(Emmanuel Geibel)

Whoever in delight would roam
Should go before the morning light:
The wood is still as a great church dome,
The little winds not yet in flight,
And still asleep, the lark, the rook,
Though in the tall green grass, the brook
Gently sings its morning rite.

The whole world's like a book whereon
Many a maxim's inscribed for us
In colorful lines wherein we're shown
Just how the Lord stays true to us.
Wood and flower near and far—
These and shining morning star
Are testaments of His love for us.

Then prayer drifts like a breath of air
Throughout one's senses, softly plays
While love knocks at the heart's mute lair
In all her sundry silent ways—
Knocks and knocks; the lair is glowing;
And one's lips are overflowing
With a noisy, jubilant praise.

And all at once the nightingale
Rings abroad from bush and sward;
The sound awakes on hill, in vale
And wants to rise in full accord
With the morning's ardent fire,
Which seems to chime now, like a gentle choir:
Let us all sing praise to the Lord!

THE BELATED WANDERER

(Joseph von Eichendorff)

Ah, but where will I be in springs to come?
Or so I asked (else at ease) when, hat a-swing,
In the vale we let our glad songs ring
And every treetop offered fresh wreaths for some.

For then I knew that spring would shine forever,
Streams ever fling their gleaming splash to the sea,
Birds ever sing from wonderlands, dreamily,
Dawn light know an ending? Never!

But evening comes; and every friend, I find,
Fatigued with roaming, has long since lagged behind.
Now, through my wilted wreaths, the night airs hum.

While bells of evening lead toward home and night,
I ask, in all my loneliness and fright:
Ah, where will I be in springs to come?

HOMECOMING

(Joseph von Eichendorff)

The winter morning shines clear and fair.
The wanderer's long been away.
Frost makes him shiver, stiffens his hair.
The lovely land lies to its prey:
"Now I'll rest here for evermore,"
He thinks as he knocks on his father's door.

Yet those who'd have opened it are dead;
Little of home's left to save.
Utter strangers eye him instead,
As if he'd come from the grave.
Feeling a chill clear down to the bone,
He flees to the fields to be alone.

Yet scarcely a bird's song rings out now
As he leans against a tree.
The lovely garden? All hacked up now.
All's like some eerie fantasy.
And hearing how the morning bells have pealed,
He sinks to his knees in the silent field.

And standing up again from prayer,
Not knowing where to turn,
He sees a youth beside him there
Who takes his hand with gentle concern:
"Come along? A short walk, then rest."
He follows, touched by this gentle request.

Now they climb as if toward the sky,
Through the dark mountain solitude;
Not one church bell can reach this high;
They watch in silent, dreary mood
As all lands fade in the bleak background
While stars bloom in the trees all around.

His guide now gently lifts his light,

36

And now by his torch they roam,
Silently through the silent night
Now widening like a dome
Built by invisible hands, and here
The wanderer's seized by a secret fear.

He speaks: What bears the wind with such force,
What sweeps up here with such strange swells,
As if I could hear distant waters course
Between the beating of bells?
"That's the sound in the heights of the song
They sing in praise of Him all night long."

The wanderer looks up. "I can't go on.
Can it be morning that blinds my eyes?
What's shining there—like cities at dawn?"
His friend waves his torch and replies:
"Now your days of unrest are past.
When you awake, we're home at last."

THE RETURN HOME

(Maria Luise Weissmann)

Perhaps the slender shaft of the birch has borne me to this maze
Where my feet take root in blackberry vines' entangled web?
Dragonflies take flight above the pale blue pond of my gaze;
Grasses in the southerly wind of my breath now flow and ebb;
And just as waves of mild air flow forth from my lips,
So does the grain field's hair of gold bow to the earth.
A dream of beetles springs out of my fingertips,
And crickets fiddle from my armpits' leaf-fringed berth.
Oh, I become expanse and depth and forest now;
My weary and laden lashes, dozing, start to fill
With green. And listen: hear how that little woodpecker, my heart,
Softly hammers toward me from a distant hill.

THE WANDERING STAFF

(Maria Luise Weissmann)

I was once Ahasver's,
Tannhäuser's too.
Turned green, took root,
Rose up, became a bush, and grew and grew.

Now the world is seeded
With my brood:
Each seedling urged
And urged that ancient, restless, raging mood.

For the sake of its power.
Seized by its soul,
He who grips me will meet
His goal as only a means to one more goal.

No house can protect
Him who takes me on.
On many roads
He roams round and round, committed to none, unknown.

Scant reapers for
The spacious mead;
It strains toward each hand—
Yes, strains quite greedily, the ripened seed:

Seeks a way that from me
It might be born
Yet just stands entrapped
And sobs beneath the whining wind, forlorn.

Mishear not the longing
Burning round you, my friend.
Grip one thing and take it:
Calm, guide it, man, on toward its end.

IN THE EVENING

(Hedwig Lachmann)

Do you know then—when, on tree and bush,
The branches tremble, rise, and fall,
And when, with gently-swelling hush,
Smoke spreads against a weather wall,

A timid bird—only half-aloud—
Beats its wings and brushes near you,
And cloud builds into larger cloud,
Where your wild, wild wish will bear you?

Well, then, do you know, when the whole world again
Snuggles by the fire so cozily,
And you're seized with longing, well, do you know then
Where your own native land might be?

AT SUNSET

(Joseph von Eichendorff)

We've roamed, both cursed and blessed,
Together, hand in hand;
From wandering, now we rest
Above the silent land.

Already dark, the skies;
The vales slope here and there;
The larks alone now rise
Dreamily in the air.

Come here. Let them play.
Soon time for bed, my dear
(To keep us from going astray
In this solitude out here).

O still, expansive peace
So deep in sunset's red!
So nice to let wandering cease;
Is to do so to be dead?

A WINTER EVENING

(Georg Trakl)

At the window now, the fall of snow.
It's long been tolling, the evening bell.
The table's set for many, as well,
The house well-ordered, all aglow.

And many from their wanderings
Arrive by dark paths at the gate.
The tree of grace blooms gold, if late;
From out of earth's chill sap it springs.

Traveler, enter with silent tread.
Pain has petrified the door.
Yet clean and bright on the table before
You gleam the wine, the bread.

ABOUT THE TRANSLATOR

William Ruleman grew up in Memphis, Tennessee, attended the University of the South at Sewanee, and received his bachelor's and master degrees in English at the Universities of Virginia and Memphis, respectively. He went on to earn the Ph.D. in English in 1994 from the University of Mississippi. Thereafter, he taught literature and writing at Tennessee Wesleyan University until his retirement in 2018.

He has translated three books by Stefan Zweig (*Vienna Spring: Early Novellas and Stories* and *Clarissa: the fragment of a novel* for Ariadne Press and *A Girl and the Weather: Poems and Prose* for Cedar Springs Books), as well as *Selected Poems* of Maria Luise Weissmann and *Early Poems* of Hermann Hesse, both published by Cedar Springs Books.

Volumes of his own poetry include *From Rage to Hope* (White Violet Books), *A Palpable Presence* and *Sacred and Profane Loves* (both from Feather Books), and, from Cedar Springs Books, *Munich Poems* and *Salzkammergut Poems*.